Inspirational Knowledge

Emmazina Day

INSPIRATIONAL KNOWLEDGE

Authorunit
17130 Van Buren Blvd., Ste. 238,
Riverside, CA 92504
877-826-5888
www.authorunit.com

ISBN 979-8-89030-097-3 (Paperback)
ISBN 979-8-89030-100-0 (Ebook)

Printed in the United States of America.

No Time To Waste ...No Time To Waste!
Be Kind Always enough said.

Contents

DEDICATION

*T*his audio book is inspirational and Knowledgeable dedicated to my family, my kids and the love I have for the Welly Bellie Kids. I'm hoping it will have an impact on someone who loves to read and listen to my audio books. My short audio stories mommy teaches me to pray are the voices of Rajah Ford and silhouette. Thank you so very much! many blessings. May I put a smile on your face today?... Welly Bellie Kids I would like to brighten your day just a little. Dear Jesus, I come to you in prayer and ask humbly will you please continue to help us to be kind to one another no matter the color of our skin. Please continue to guide us and the right direction and do your will. And Jesus name I pray amen.

ACKNOWLEDGEMENT

Become a warrior for the Lord.

The Lord, said …

Well Done

Good and faithful servant, you have been faithful over few things. I will make thee ruler over many things.

(Matthew 25:21)

Hello Wellie Bellie Kids of all ages,

Our heavenly Father wants us all to draw Close to him, God knows our circumstances, he is closer than we think, we just need to keep praying to him, no matter what. No matter how busy we think we are, make a little time for him. As we know it has been written that Jesus died on the cross for all our sins. Only Jesus can bring you peace. This is what we all need. We are all living in sad times right now with the pandemic, we need Jesus more than we ever thought we needed him before. We all have a teardrop in our hearts, Everyday someone loses a loved one far or near, on a daily basis… Procast News we hear brings us such sadness... I must say we need laughter. The sound of happiness is desperately needed around the world. It is necessary for us to have this communication, to keep us safe and to give us knowledge. Let's keep our heads up and continue to pray. Many blessings in this New Year 2021.

Happy New Year !!! Please stay safe, happy, stay in love, find peace in your heart always.

God bless

Blessings

Author: Emmazina Day

LOVING ME FIRST

I've always heard loving me first. Is the first rule...

Self preservation is the first law of nature.

Take care of me first, then I can help take care of others...
How about you?

LET'S BE HAPPY

$\mathcal{W}$e chose to sleep in anger instead of in each other's arms. You and I. We chose each other for better or for worse. We were supposed to love each other, and walked together, in life and started a new beginning. Instead, we chose to leave and take a different path. Until death due us part. We chose to fight instead of making love, we both let nightfall… fall on us. With a frown upon our face. Instead of making up. We chose to be miserable in darkness, before the twilight of dawn. While the stars were shining so bright before the sunrise, we still had anger in our hearts. We chose to have a free-spirited husband and wife. We chose this, you and I. We chose to live in peace. We chose to love each other apart. Now we soar like two, Doves. Free. We chose this for you and me.

TODAY TOMORROW AND ALWAYS

$\mathcal{P}$eople, change how they think and do things in life all the time. Sometimes just to try and fit in. Teenagers try, at times to be someone they are not, may be with a bad attitude, mood swings, maybe some sort of a hardship has happen. Whatever life may have thrown at you. You have to understand, life mishaps, happens to us all. What can you do? or what do you need to do? try this say a little prayer or whisper Jesus name, to redirect your mind, God, will always be with us because he lives within us all. You do not try to be someone you are not.

Our Father, is in heaven and he always stay the same. Today tomorrow and always. Trust his word, His promise is true he can not lie. Jesus, loves us unconditionally, his ways of thinking, is not our way of thinking."

I'm Just sayin...

PRAYING

$\mathcal{L}$et me say this, we all know it does not cost you anything to pray. But this is the way king Jesus tells us all to pray. To communicate, tell him how you feel, and what you need,not so much what you want. Even though God already knows everything about us all . God is our creator. He still wants us all to pray and believe. Let's acknowledge him and give thanks. It costs you nothing, it's free.

LET'S WALK AND TALK

If you feel a soft and warm breeze brush so softly across your face. Your entire body feels the warmth of love. That›s God embracing you. God is letting you know he's with you just listen, be still for a few minutes, you can feel him, close by. listen to his soft-spoken message God is giving you. Close your eyes, for a moment think about being at peace, asking We are so caught up asking for what we want or what we need. Let's ask him. How he's doing. Let's walk and talk to see what God is saying to us, you're walking, on a beach. On a sunny Sunday morning. The sun is just coming up, the sand is so warm to the touch of your feet. You feel so carefree you feel so blessed. To have this wonderful feeling, of the warmth of the sun on your body. The colors are so heavenly in the sky mixed with blue, yellow, red, and orange, so beautiful to the eye. So peaceful to hear the sounds of the ocean. The waves, you see a glare over the ocean, you feel the warmth of love all over you. So much peace so quiet, a voice inside within, you, God, is saying. I will never leave you. I love you so much. When you see a rainbow in the sky, It's a reminder of a promise God made to you so long ago. I will never leave you, I'm always close to your heart.

HEALING HANDS

*T*hank you father, for giving me the patients, to come to work, with a gentle smile, healing hands to help. To be able to help others. Jesus walked with me. Give me the right words to say to encourage someone with a broken spirit, that awaits on my return to use my strength to help when they know longer have the will power or strength to stand or walk. Father gives me healing hands to touch someone and a gentle way. To give comfort and compassion to their ailing bodies, I ask this and Jesus' name, to help me show love, and allow me to have a listening ear. Father gives me patients, when I need it the most, to continue my daily duties. Father, hear my prayer, I need you!

RECIPE

*F*or Jesus Love
Ingredients:
One cup of Faith
Four cups of laughter
Five cups of forgiveness
Half cup of recognize

Two cups of love

Ok let's get started ...to add faith we need a mustard seed of faith one cup should do it. Let's add : Forgiveness the bible says forgive each other, just as Jesus forgave us ! Just in case someone sins against you. Alright, got it. Now what?, let's see, add: Two cups of Laughter boy we need these ingredients yes! We do need a whole heap. Ok what's next.

Two cups of Love, ok Jesus loves us unconditionally like our parents do right.? It's in there ok next. Half of cup of Recognize Jesus, Is our ingredient to love and he forgives us of our sins and with his love brings laughter, of peace and puts a smile on our face. All we have to do is Recognize and have the faith to keep believing our Heavenly Father is always there for us. That's a lot of ingredients... yep! Try Jesus.

MASK

The world we live in today is not healthy, please everyone listen, wear your mask! or some kind of face covering. It's so important to do so. More than I can emphasize, wash your hands using hand sanitizer as much as possible. Hospitals at this time are overwhelmed in some areas, why wait to get this vicious virus that has killed so many. young and old, this virus does not have a preference, anyone at any age can get very sick Whatever your preference is take care of YOU!

We Need Jesus!

DEAR MOTHER

*W*ith a warm hug and a kind smile, she says to me her nurse. I'm ninety-nine and a half I'm old why am I still here I do not want to be a burden to my family or anyone my family found a place for me I'm weak and I'm weary I no longer can take care of myself my family has families of their own I wonder why I am still here at 99 and 1/2 Dear Jesus what do I have to offer at my age to anyone I am sick and I'm ready to be with you. My family takes me to this place. My kids tell me mother this is your new home. I see lots of smiley faces and all I can think of is I do not want to be here. I heard all kinds of stories about places like this. Some good and some bad I hear a voice that says welcome. I'm your nurse. She says to me you're more valuable than a diamond, you are my mother, my grandmother. You're family when you enter into this facility you became a part of this family we are here to take care of you it's better than being home in a way all you need to do is tell us what you need or what you want we will do our best to take care of you so you see Mother you gained a daughter a son and grandchildren. You're precious to us. We are special people we take care of your needs we are angels on earth I say thank you Dear Jesus for allowing us to take care of someone who's 99 1/2 years old, without you where would we be you have the knowledge you can share if you like, as we will listen to your good times we will listen to your bad time after all you have been here ninety-nine and a half years Jesus has a plan for you. Your work here on earth is not quite done you see you cannot leave us just yet until God calls you home I know you're weak I know you're tired but you are a mother you are a grandmother you are a daughter you are a sister you are family you are blessed you are a woman who gave birth to plenish the earth a woman's work is never done they say without you where would we be. So you see mother keep the faith, keep sharing, keep praying, keep giving us the knowledge of the Lord even at 99 and a half you are priceless to us all, never feel you have nothing to offer. You have given us a lifetime of love so we say thank you, Mom! Now it's our time to take care of you.

We love you Mother always and forever.

HUSH YOUR MOUTH

*W*e need to be careful of what we say. What you say, can and will be harmful. We need to understand what it means, to say things out of our mouth, that's not cool. Like using profanity. We should not say certain things, because our life is being recorded just like everything else in this world. It's not what I'm saying... it's what the bible tells us. we just need to read and pay attention, and listen to what is the right things to say ...I'm just saying, it's very easy to get caught up and before you know it "Bam!" we have said some slick stuff out of our mouth, it's hard to say the right things, all the time. It's very hard, but like they say nothing comes easy in this world. For most of us. We do have rules to follow, they are called the ten commandments.

The bible says God said so. Just saying.

{ Matthew 12:36 }

GRANDMA TALKING

*G*randma is talking red, yellow black and white we are Priceless in his sight. God loves us all. All the children in this world. God tells us to watch, believe in him and have faith, be brave, be strong and all that we do, let it be done with love. Rainbow Babies read your Bibles or ask Mom and Dad to read a Bible verse to you. I love you so very much you know, no one always does good, you know why ? because we were born with sin now wait a minute God will forgive you for your sins if you pray and ask for forgiveness and do not do it again sometimes it is not easy to do but we must try as hard as we can God gave us rules to live by and they are called The Ten Commandments we must we should obey God's rules. Now listen to Nolan Cierra, Adonia, Saniaya, Tavion, Jakyla, Jayden and Jayceon! be quiet, sit still and I'm going to read you the Ten Commandments. The first commandment is 1. Thou shall have no other Gods before me 2. Thou shall not make unto thee any Graven image or any likeness of any thing that is in heaven above or that is under the Earth beneath or that is in the waters 3. Thy shall bow down that self to them nor serve them for the Lord that God is a jealous God. 4.Thou shall not take the name of the Lord thy God in vain for the Lord will not hold him Guiltless that taketh his name in vain. five. remember the Sabbath day to keep it holy 6. Honor thy father and a mother that their days may be long upon the land which the Lord thy God giveth thee 7.Thou shall not kill 8. Thou shall not commit adultery 9. Thou shall not steal. 10. Thou shall not bear false witness against thy neighbor. when you Weallie Bellie kids, when you kids can read on your own I would like you to learn the

Ten Commandments. You can read this in the King James version in the Holy Bible Exodus 20. We are not perfect so never think you will not make mistakes or do wrong because you will. This is what we call Life Jesus want us to live on this Earth be happy and in good health this is what the Bible tells us there for what a belly kids be good listen to your parents learn to pray and say your prayers at night get into the habit of saying your prayers at night as you grow you will not forget to pray. Jesus is always listening. Jesus can see you but you cannot see him; he is like the wind. You cannot see the wind but we can feel it right? God lives in each one of our hearts, if we follow the ten commandments one day we will see Jesus. Jehovah God promises that one day we will see him again Jesus left to go back to heaven to prepare a place for us. God's name is Jehovah! That's Jesus' father. God loves us unconditionally now Wellie Bellie kids that's all for now. Now give Grandma a great big hug if your parents or someone you care about are reading this story to you say thank you! give them a big hug too. God bless you babies grandma loves you all.

THE SLANTED EYE

*T*his little girl named Pebbles was having a sad day and decided to go to the park she thought by going to the park she would feel better but she did not she looked up and she saw there was an old lady with a big blue hat on and dark sunglasses sitting on the bench at the park feeding the Ducks the old lady and returned look at the Young Pebbles 10 or 11 years old sitting with tears rolling down her cheeks feeling sad unpretty actually, she thought she was ugly but Pebbles was a very beautiful young girl Pebbles had only one problem she has a slanted eye. She was born with this condition, called Duane syndrome sometimes kids were born with this condition but for Pebbles, she did not like it at all she felt she was different from all the other kids sometimes they made fun of her but her mother had taught her sticks and stones may break your bones but words can never hurt you, but still, she secretly felt sad Pebbles thinking what could be done about her eye the old woman with the blue hat decided to walk over to see what was wrong with young Pebbles the old lady said hello little one what seems to have you so sad the old woman asked. Pebbles, answer no one wants to be my friend because I'm different, the young Pebble answered. You do not look any different from anyone else I see or know.

Ms. Gottado said Pebbles. Pebbles answer I am! look at me look at my eye! the old woman said my name is Ms. Gottado, what kind of name is that!? Ms.Gottado says I have to do what I got to do! wow! said Pebble that's different... the old lady says ...Pebbles I do not sit around and think what people think of me people can be very cruel Jesus made me as I am so I am beautiful the way I am despite what people think to let this be a lesson it's more important to be beautiful from the inside than the outside pretty is ..as pretty does but some people would think differently we all have our own opinion Ms. Gottado said what is your name Pebbles my name is Pebbles and the old woman smiled and said like The Flintstones? Pebbles says yes well Pebbles the old woman said it's time for me to go now. I enjoy talking with you I have to go now and do what I got to do so the old woman stood up took off her sunglasses and looked at Pebbles and she smiled and said you see you are not so different my dear my eye is slanted too so cheer up my dear and you do what you gotta do God bless you my child and Pebbles turned her head and looked away thinking about what the old lady had just said and when Pebbles turned her head back to look at Ms. Gottado.

Ms. Gottado was gone! Pebbles just turned her head for a second. She wanted to thank the old woman for taking the time to talk with her. Pebbles did not know Ms. Gottado was her guardian angel watching over her. It's nice to know we all have a guardian angel.

Luke 22:43 and there appear in angel.

THE FAVOR

*O*nly God can give you a favor. He can make a way out of no way. Jesus, can fill your life full of faith, if you only believe in him. Surrender yourself, Jesus loves you! God has given you good health, love, peace of mind, a mother and father to instill good values. Everything we have comes from God. Only the king can give you peace with favor, all we have is right now. Almighty God, promise this! Whenever we see a rainbow, it's a reminder to let us know Jesus will be back one day. The gifts of favor.

DEAR JESUS

*M*y mom and dad are not together anymore they both say they love me but I'm not sure I live with my mommy she likes to party and have her friends over at home, all the time we don't do anything together like we used to do when Dad was here my mommy takes drugs when I'm in school I learned to stay away from drugs my mommy got in trouble because of her addiction we are so poor in my mom she isn't a good housekeeper either I had to wear dirty clothes to school mommy would rush me out the house without taking a bath, I don't want the kids to make fun of me. I am just so sad. Jesus, I was in school and my teacher said that I could not go back home for a while have to stay with some other people I do not know but they will treat me very nicely. I want my daddy! What am I going to do? I'm only six years old! I want my daddy right please call my dad! I want my Nana! She lives far away in another state. Far away from here, I'm sure she will come and get me I am her princess I do not want to stay with people I do not know I want my own family I'm so sad Jesus Ms. Jackson, the lady I must stay with, says your Daddy has to go to court and talk with the judge before you can go home, Dear Jesus please let my daddy and Nana come to get me so I will not be so sad. I remember my Nana saying princess God is always with us and we all have a guardian angel watching over us. I began to feel better. My

Daddy went to court but I could not go to court, I'm only six years old. Dear Jesus, there was a knock on the door. It was my daddy! I was so happy to see my daddy. I said thank you, Jesus! For sending my daddy to get me I thank my guardian angel too. Ms. Jackson was not so bad after all, I said thank you, Miss Jackson! For caring for me dad says we are a family and family who pray together stay together and I believe him. Jesus, thank you for loving me. Amen

FISHER'S HILL

*F*isher Hill is known to us children as the Ponderosa where our grandparents lived for over 40 years. Every summer we kids get together for the summer and we have lots of fun. Our grandparents had ten children and our parents had 8 or 10 kids. We had a large family, it was a lot of us we had lots of sisters brothers and cousins to play with we had all kinds of ideas but not many toys to play with after all we are at Grandma's house and there was always something to do if we could not find anything to do grandma could. They lived on a farm and grew everything you can imagine to eat watermelon, cantaloupe corn, collard greens ,sweet peas butter beans, cabbage squash tomatoes and lots more. They even had an apple tree and a grapevine with the biggest sweetest grapes. We loved to eat them so much. Grandma prepared all our food fresh. She loves to cook for us kids. I loved her fresh baked bread. I would wake up to the smell of fresh country bacon and pop and hot biscuits homemade not from the can. The smell of love. I would always say I'm so happy to be at Grandma's house! my grandad was always around but we kids for some reason would always say it's Grandma's house that is just what we like to say guess what? Behind Grandma's house there is a graveyard. A big ten fence was the only thing that kept us kids out! we were curious but we wasn't allowed to play in the graveyard Randy Bunkie my cousins and I would come to visit and often talked about going into the graveyard not me I would say to my cousin honey honey she was the quiet one she just listen to all the stories I will tell her about all of us Betty Boo live down the street from my grandparents house she was my cousin too we kids would race down to Betty Boo's house to see who could run the fastest I would be somewhere in the middle the boys always out ran the girls we would say you boys always cheat! the boys would give us a head start they still won! Bunkie got bored easily and he said let's go play in the graveyard he was always getting into trouble this particular day all of us kids was visiting Grandma when grown folks talk we kids had to go in another room or outside if the weather permits the weather permitted we all headed to the backyard honey honey Randy Bunkie Gina Bina BettyBoo and me Toosieroll, we kids all peeped over the big ten fence I was the one who was always scared of everything but I decided to climb over the fence with the rest of my cousin's we all got over the fence okay we stood up on a log just looking out at the Tombstones all broken this cemetery needed a lot of work . so it looks like it was forgotten,we started walking and looking at the names on the tombes they where dated back to the 800's I said wow! these people were old. I wonder where they liked us when they were children. I feel like we should not be here but at the same time I felt like we should do something that needed to be done. This graveyard had been forgotten where were the families? oh yeah... I guess they were all gone too. My cousins were walking and some were running looking all around but they were very quiet. I wonder if they were thinking the same thing I was. Ooooh I hear grandma calling we had better get back or we all are going to be in serious trouble Gwen said Bunkie this is all your fault! He laughed and we all started back over the fence. Grandma was still calling us. We could not leave honey honey, she was the youngest one. She started to cry. Gwen I could not get back over the fence grandma was still calling us but we could not leave honey honey she was the youngest one she started crying. Gwen was the strong one. She said don't cry, I will help you... I was trying to get across myself but I kept falling backwards and it was easy getting across this fence but hard getting back I remember wait a minute we had something to stand on to get over the fence what was us girls thinking Randy and bunkie hopped over the fence and they went back to Grandma's house when they looked back and did not see us they started back to help. Grandma called again and they were both out of breath. Grandma asked where have you boys been and we're are the girls. We all were in big trouble now I knew we were going to be punished. Bunkie said Grandma, they're still trying to catch their breath. He said they were just playing grandma... Go get them girls and tell them to come inside to eat right now you could tell that in her voice she was somewhat upset with us. We were only six and seven years old. From the south. We ran back as fast as we could the boys came back to help us girls back across the face. We said that was a close one. We all said Dear Jesus thank you so much for watching over us and keeping us safe. Gwen, asked Bunkie what did you tell Grandma he said the truth Gwen! she said what! you never tell the truth Bunkie, says to Gwen, we all were playing this what I said to Grandma. Bunkie said grandma asked us to come get you girls so we did we all started giggling and we thought we had got away with something, thinking back going into the graveyard was not good to do. Grandma looked at us and she said you Wellie Bellie kids have been playing in the graveyard. We were shocked! we did not know what to say but we should have known Grandma sees everything and she knows everything she says it's her job to know she was so upset and she looked at each one of us and she said so what did you think when you were doing the wrong things and you kids knew better you knew not to go into the graveyard someone could have gotten hurt no one said anything I Toosieroll my big mouth said Grandma we need to do something to help those people grandma said Toosieroll there isn›t anything we can do for them they live on this earth a long time ago no grandma I mean can we do something to fix the cemetery up grandma says you mean can we clean up the cemetery? we can ask around and see if we can get volunteers who would like to help with a project like this first we have to get permission from the city to do this is a good idea Tootsie Roll it does not change the fact you kids did not listen I am glad no one got hurt but yes something does need to be done you Wellie Bellie kids have to stop being so curious and all of you kids are on punishment! when the ice cream truck comes by your kids will not be allowed to get any ice cream. Tootsie Roll do not look at me with those sad eyes you still not getting any ice cream I want you kids to think about what you did the wrong grandmother says dear Jesus thank you for watching over my grandchildren why they were in mischief. Amen.

PRAYING

𝒫raying cost you nothing praying is very easy to do close your eyes put your hands together and start talking to Jesus tell him how you feel inside tell him that you're thankful for all the wonderful things he has done for you and others we have so much to be grateful for and we need to tell God how we really feel inside we have to feed our soul with the word of our savior Jesus Christ Wellie Bellie kids you should always remember you're not alone always remember you do have someone you can talk too no matter what time, it's okay any time you want! fill your bellies up with the knowledge of God and you will have a whale of a bellie! and that's why I call you babies my Wellie Bellie kids learn all you can about Jesus Christ, Jesus is just like food you need him to fill your spiritual hunger for our heavenly Father.

LET YOUR HEART NOT BE TROUBLE

$\mathcal{L}$et your heart not be troubled believe in God Yea..believe in God also in me. In my father's house there are many mansions. If it were not so I would have told you. I go to prepare a place for you and if I go and prepare a place for you I will come again and receive you unto myself that where I am there ye may be also.

John 14 1:3

MOMMY SAYS....

*G*od tell us Jesus loves us Jesus want us to be his friend he want us to talk to him daily Jesus says I'm here I'm listening to your heart I feel your pain I died for you because I love you so much bring all your worries to me in prayer my child only I can give you peace yes Jesus loves you for the Bible tells us so.

NEVER STOP LOVING JESUS

*N*ever stopped loving life ...life... is a gift from our father Jehovah God and his son Jesus Christ never stopped loving your neighbor your neighbor is anyone not just the people next door where you live the Bible tell us to love our neighbor even if we never took the time to say hello do so please you never know your strength that God has given you until you have been put to the test never stop thanking Jesus for your gift of life... life ...what a privilege to have an awesome God who forgives us for all our sins we cannot be anything but grateful for this who are we ? to complain about anything there is nothing without good health and someone to love and someone you can love back... Our father in Heaven loves us always ...Jesus tell us that he has gone to prepare a place for us in that there are many mansions. What a blessing!

John 14-1:3

PUTTING GOD FIRST

*W*hen you are putting Jesus first in your life he will guide your daily day and night because when King Jesus has his arms around you the world cannot do you any harm when you're feeling blue or you're not feeling well calling your heavenly father okay he has been so good to you he's able to wake you up this morning so you can go to school so you can play with y'all I passed your computer's visit your friends if you are 18 or older Jesus is helping you prepare for work today and everyday just allows you to go on with your daily lives Jesus has been so good to you always remember Jesus died for us on the cross I know we get so busy and sometimes forget to pray for me as soon as you remember do so because when we need Jesus we want him to put us further don't we but we are sick we call on Jesus when we are in pain and we no longer can bury we call on Jesus any life problems we feel we can not handle the call almost had to be there for us and I need all the Jesus asking for us is to talk to him pray talking to your friend helps relieve the stress of daily living but you're not sure you want ever hear it again. God has a listening ear you will not hear again, whatever you share with God it's private. but Jesus will carry you when you are weak he will never leave your side the Bible tells us that Jesus cannot lie!

WE NEED JESUS!

*W*e need to call on our Heavenly Father Jehovah God and his son Jesus Christ all given times. In the morning and in the evening anytime you feel you want to talk you can! you do not need an appointment to talk to our heavenly father he's listening to you. When we are happy talk when we are sad talk ! you do not have to stand in a line and you do not have to have money he is My Greatest Inspiration you can have a very good conversation with Jesus in your mind that this is a very special conversation because no one knows what you are playing Jesus loves you unconditionally never feel that God do not love or care about you because he does he cannot lie we can talk to each other about our problems we forget. add time for Fears sometimes to pray because we are so busy focusing on our own problem we think we can fix that problem. We should hold I hear it's up for about a headstand put your hands together and pray to our Heavenly Father swelly belly kids take all your problems to God In Prayer Jehovah is our creator and he knows us better than anyone tell someone about Jesus today read your Bible listen to your parents share your knowledge with someone you love okay we all need Jesus.

RECOGNIZE

*W*e need to recognize love, when we see it! love comes in all shapes and sizes. Why wait to let the other person know. How much you really care? Grandmom!

We care we love you, family and friends listen! we all need to show love to one another. Almighty God, blessed us to love and care for each other. When someone we love is helpless or sick . We need to recognize, and not wait until they are no longer with us. Or to say I love you.

But we are quick to say, ok well I'm going to call you but I forgot. I just got so busy working and I just forgot. You may even say just… So much going on… I haven›t had the time. And I just forgot. I just had no time to to show love… There are so many excuses we use. Mother, I was so tired and I was going to stop by to see you. It's just been one thing or another that's keeping me from visiting. We do not mean any harm, we all just get caught up, and our own daily lives, so busy we all are. We just forget at times, to take the time, out to say…

I Love You. To the ones who mean, the most to us. We weren't too busy to say, Mother or Grandma, can you, will you take me to the mall or drop me off at the movies… whatever the reason is Grandma, Mother, or Dad was always there with open arms a loving smile. she or he may say ok come on… let's go… you guys do not make any sense. But guess what Recognize. She took the time out for you! she never said I'm too busy, I just forgot! please stop being so busy, get off the cell phones, get off the computer. Stop. Take a moment and say I Love

You! Mom. Would you like to take a walk in the park or just sit and talk? It doesn't cost you anything to call or visit, with a kind word or a hug. Let's say or do something. Your choice but do something memorable, with the one who means something to you. Recognize love when it's right in front of you!

Recognize

ONE WINTER NIGHT

*W*hen Bella was a little girl, Late one cold night she awoke to the warmth of her feet on the bedroom floor. Bella said to herself my feet feel so wonderfully warm on the floor it seem to be just the right temperature for Bella, little feet.

There was no carpet on the wood floors. The floor was so warm that Bella›s feet were almost too hot. But strangely enough just right, She was always cold. She had no socks to keep her feet warm. Mom had so many kids, and not enough food or clothes we wore hand me downs meaning when they get too small for you pass them down to your siblings, but you had to take care of the clothes so they will be nice for your sisters. Bella headed to the bathroom. There was not a little night light for her to see during her nightly visits, Bella could see around the room in the dark because the light from outside the window gave her some light and she saw her own shadow. Outside' her window was a street light that comes on every night at 9:00 sharp.

Bella has gotten up so many times before but this time it was different. Something was wrong. She felt danger and smelled smoke. She opened her bedroom door and knocked on her Mother's door. She came to the door and saw the smoke and she said Bella,! run next door and knock on the neighbor's door, keep knocking until someone comes to the door and tell them to call for help!!! It's 2:00 am Bella did exactly as her mother asked her to do. With no shoes on, no coat on. Bella was only eight years old but she was very smart, she was the oldest of eight children. She had learned a lot at a young age to help her mother. Mother has been teaching her to help out. It was freezing outside. A little light snow that just covered the ground This is an emergency Bella, thought to herself. When she got outside she could see the flames coming from the back of the house where she had just used the restroom. Bella, started to pray Jesus help my family to safety please. Please father, Do not let them burn in this old cold house. with the cold floors. Bella was only a little girl. So much to take in but she learned so much about safety. When she saw the red flashing lights, neighbors all around her came out of their homes to help. Bella didn't see her Mom! she panicked and started to call out Mommy! Mommy!! The neighbor held Bella close to her, giving her motherly love. Bella just wanted to run into her mother's arms. Bella's mom came out of the burning house with her little brother and sister. It was such a joy for Bella, to see her family and to know they all were ok. Mother came and stood by Bella with her step Dad, when she heard mommy say where is my baby? Lulla-by Bella's step Dad took off running the man with the fire suit on and said it's too late, no one can go back in the burning house, well her stepfather took off running and went back inside despite what he was told. What a courageous Dad! oh my goodness the fear we all had for what seemed like such a long time but it was only minutes... here comes Bella's step dad with baby Lulla-by, in his arms. Know one was injured.

Thank you Jesus! What a joy to see her baby sister Lulla-by, she is a beautiful baby girl. She had no idea what was going on. Lulla-by was only six months old. such danger she was in. God's mercy and grace had saved Lulla-bye, Bella and her whole family were saved. The power of a small prayer from Bella saying

Thank you Jesus... Amen

There is a place where your fingerprints still rest.
Your kisses still linger, and your whisper still softly
echos, in my ear. It's the place where a part of you
will forever be a part of me, your heart.

SHEENA

$\mathcal{I}$t's time for bed do not forget to brush your teeth and brush your hair let Mommy know when you are ready to say your prayers Mommy I do not know how to pray well let's see what God says kneel and put your hands together little one close your eyes our father who is in heaven Hallowed be thy name your Kingdom come you will be done on Earth as it is in heaven give us this day our daily bread and forgive us our adepts as we forgive our debtors lead us not into temptation but deliver us from evil for thou is the kingdom and the power and the glory forever amen.

MOTHER AND DAUGHTER'S LOVE

A Mother's love for her daughter. Is a love, you cannot describe. When a mother loves you, she loves you unconditionally, she's there for your every whim, every tear that falls. You can count on your mother. To be there for her daughter. A daughter loves her Mother with so much love, she respects her and she's proud to be her daughter.

Mother is there to talk to her daughter, when she's older. And she really needs Mother, Daughter realize Mother can wipe away her tears, from her cheeks. Put a loving smile on her face.

Mother will take all her worries and frustrations, away by sitting you down for a nice home cooked meal made just the way you like it. A glass of your favorite beverage and feel your heart up with wisdom, the tone of her voice will ease the tear you have shared with Mom. Mother, will Listen to you with whatever you have on your mind. will then look at you and say everything will be alright my daughter, with a smile only a mother can give, you hear her voice and you just know you're ok. Mother is always called Mom. Or mommy, There are known words to say, because Mom's will say whatever she feels her heart needs to say to her child whether it's right or wrong we listen to Mom. We do not follow her advice, at times. We grow weak, when we stray away. Sometimes we do not listen to Mom, when she speaks knowledge into our hearts. Are we listening? Sometimes, we are and sometimes not. Some of us daughters act like we have all the answers and we do not. Not realizing how much of this knowledge she's trying to relay to us, is very important to our hearts and mind. Until you're much older. Then we realize, Jesus says. honor your mother and your Father and your days shall be long upon the land.

A mother is a strong woman whose love has no ending for her children. No matter what age, they may become. Mother can feed you, like she feeds her baby, Without having a bottle. Or having to wash a bottle. As you get older, she will still feed you with advice. She will never sugar coat the truth this is the way God has made a woman. A woman with soft skin and soft hands. When she looks into your eyes. She means what she says. And she says what she means.

Almighty God, knew exactly what he was doing, when he made a woman, called Mother. One thing we know we can not live on this earth, without a woman called Mother.

Cherish your Mom always.

DR. JESUS

*W*hat a beautiful name! What a powerful name Jesus! What a name we all should know the name is.

Dr. Jesus! Can anyone think of a time when you needed Jesus? When Jesus was not there for you. He's always in the midst of all things. I promise you he's there for you. Pray and ask your heavenly father whatever you need from him. Take it all to Jesus... The bible tells us God died for our sins and he did. So I love to call Jesus names, Jesus sweet Jesus!... The bible tells us Jesus is coming back one day. I don't know when but he's coming. Just read the book of revelation. Read the bible for yourself, it's in there, just saying. Jesus is a jealous God, he loves for us all to pray to him. Call him in the morning, call him in the evening there's no charge to ask or talk to Dr. Jesus. Do not turn Jesus away. You do not want your soul to be lost. Jesus can fix every problem and heal every pain. Come on, let's bless his name. I'm Just saying.

INSPIRATIONAL WORDS

*J*ust saying'... Is my way of writing inspirational words to teenagers, and young adults. Who may be interested, in reading inspiring words, for a broken heart, or whatever you may be facing and life. Almighty God, will always make away for you. Prayer is the key, Just talk to him. He has helped so many people many times. I can not count the times he has saved so many lives. The most high is there, for you as well. Keep your head up.

Just saying...

CAN'T CHANGE A THANG!

*W*e can not go back, in our past. And change anything... But we can certainly start life over. By looking forward, to a new beginning. Starting now. If you wish to, move forward. Keep almighty God, first. in your life, trust and him, Your be happy you did. Believe in the living God. Victory is mine saith the lord he's waiting to hear from you.

Just sayin...

WHY YA'LL

$\mathcal{W}$hy does Love hurt?

Why do we fall in love to get hurt?

Why do we listen to the negative energy? Ladies, ladies! and gentlemen, guard your hearts. Relaxed and let go ...of the hurt, Our Father in heaven wants us to be happy and have a love for each other just like Adam and Eve. Be mindful of our newfound love. Love is... And can be very beautiful we all need that special someone in our lives. To love and care for. Just saying...

YOUR SMILE

When you smile, I smile back. Your smile is so warm and inviting. So contagious I must say. Your smile is medication to my heart. Your smile brings joy to my life. Having you in my life brings me so much happiness, so many precious memories of yesteryears. When I hear your voice, it makes my eyes sparkle and my body dance. It just reminds me of your smile, and you know when you smile. I smile back!

I'm Just saying...

Messages Of Love Dear Jesus

- Love is God
- Love is respect for each other
- Love is being in love
- Love is tears of joy
- Love is so deep it never dies
- Love is so powerful
- Love is true
- Love is so real
- Love is peace
- Love is forever
- Love is family
- Love is a feeling
- Love is a gift from heaven

Love has no words to explain

Love is Dear Jesus he died for you and I.

NEVER STOP LOVING JESUS

$\mathcal{N}$ever stopped loving life ...life... is a gift from our father Jehovah God and his son Jesus Christ never stopped loving your neighbor your neighbor is anyone not just the people next door where you live the Bible tell us to love our neighbor even if we never took the time to say hello do so please you never know your strength that God has given you until you have been put to the test never stop thanking Jesus for your gift of life... life ...what a privilege to have an awesome God who forgives us for all our sins we cannot be anything but grateful for this who are we ? to complain about anything there is nothing without good health and someone to love and someone you can love back... Our father in Heaven loves us always ...Jesus tell us that he has gone to prepare a place for us in that there are many mansions. What a blessing!

John 14-1:3

WE HAVE A SPECIAL KIND OF LOVE

*W*e have something special here. This time we're going to do it right. It takes two, not three, but two! We have what it takes to make it work. Just put God first. Secondly, put our love before anything else. I think this will only make our love stronger with passion, just the two of us, short and sweet. Let's keep our love and faith together. That's why God says when he joins a man and a woman together.

MY PURPLE TREE

*T*he Garden of love is the color of purple for me. The color of purple is love for me The color of purple is just right for two.

The color purple is the color of Royalty. It's so beautiful so magical and so spiritual the color purple is love.and so spiritual the color purple is love.

God grant me the serenity to accept the things I cannot change.

The courage to change the things I can. And the wisdom to know the different.

Written by author : Reinhold Niebuhr

I love this Prayer

MY BABY

$\mathcal{I}$n my thoughts of you there is an underlying.

Love, that is present in every word, every glimpse of every day.

I hope you feel love as I do. For it is what I feel when I'm with you. Forever you will be my love, my babe, my heart my everything.

THE BEST LIFE EVER

*T*here is always a way out of any situation. If for any reason you feel lonely or depressed, Just remind yourself God is on the throne, You know you are so blessed, to be loved by our heavenly father. This is the best gift ever! It's called "life" given to the human race. To have someone to love you so much that he would die for us all. Not only one race, but all humanity. Jesus only asked us to have faith and believe in him. He will not make or force you to love him.

God is awesome and there is nothing impossible for God to do. When you feel you are lost or in trouble. You need grace and mercy. You want God, to fight your battles, call on the King! His angels will. Try the King. He is there with open arms. Just pray and keep praying. Don't just stop praying after one or two times and then give up on Jesus. There is power in prayer. God is watching and listening. He is always on time. His time is not our time. "Try God" I'm just saying...

DEAR FATHER

I come to you in prayer for guidance. I need you in my life always Jesus. I need you to help me father, to show me the right things to do before I turn to make a wrong decision in this stressful world. Dear Jesus, only you can take away the pain and stress of everyday living I endure in life. I come to you father and prayer when I'm in pain, I call on you. Father for all my needs. I need you to help me step by step, and the name of Jesus I pray. Amen

FOREVER MINE

*F*orever my love is gone." Forever you will be missed. No more will you be by my side, but you will forever live in my heart. You will Reside in my memory forever. I think of you each and every day. I can not see you, I can know longer hear your laughter. Nor can I feel your touch. You see," God took you in peace. No more pain, no more bills. No more worries. and no more tears. I have a teardrop of sadness. For all of these things, I say they are true you see. My heart has a twinkle of a beat of happiness. I have a sadness on my face, just knowing more suffering will come again one day. But in my heart I know you're at peace, with the joy of knowing, no more pain Rest in peace my love rest in peace. Forever mine you will always be. Forever and ever. I am so grateful. God allowed our paths to meet my love. Forever mind.

*If you believe, you will receive
whatever you ask for in prayer
Matthew 21:22*

TO LOVE A FRIEND

*I*t's impossible to find good friends. It's like finding a needle in a broomstick. When you do find a best friend, they live forever in your heart. True friends are so difficult, so impossible to let go. Best friends will stick by you no matter what, my ride and die.

Friends are forever. Jesus, shows you their loyalty, their friendship and also shows you their love.

Hold on to your best friends.

Hold on to your dear friends. full of laughs, always keep a smile on your face, they keep you happy. To love a friend is to be a true friend.

9 798890 300669